Paleo Smo(
67 Delicious Gluten Free
For Weight Loss And a

(The Paleolithic Diet Desserts – Stop Sugar
the Paleo Approach)

Copyright © 2014 by Annette Goodman

All rights reserved. No part of this publication may be reproduced, stored in a retrieval system, or transmitted, in any form or by any means, electronic, mechanical, photocopying, recording or otherwise without the prior written permission of the author and the publishers.

Table of Contents

@

<u>My Mailing list</u>: If you would like to receive **new Kindle reads** on **wellness, gluten free diet, social dynamics, psychology, career, NLP, success and healthy living** for **FREE** (or deeply **discounted – as low as $0,99**) I <u>invite you to my Mailing List.</u> Whenever my new book is out, I set the promotional price/free period for two days. You will get an e-mail notification and will **be the first to get the book for $0,99 (or free)** during its limited promotion.

Why would I do this when it took me countless hours to write these e-books?

First of all, that's my way of saying **"thank you"** to my new readers. Second of all – **I want to spread the word about my new books and ideas.** Mind you that **I hate spam and e-mails that come too frequently** - no worries about that.

If you think that's a good idea and are in, just follow this link:

http://eepurl.com/R_UhP

<u>Introduction</u> Why Paleo?

The Paleo-diet is the best way to lose weight and keep it off. Once you start you will never try another fad diet again. Say goodbye to disappointment and failure and hello to success! Paleolithic living allows our bodies to function as they were designed to. You will be eating the proper foods that the body needs to operate efficiently; weight loss and health will be yours!

I have found success in the Paleolithic lifestyle and would like to share with you what I have learned. The paleo-diet is the number one way to lose weight, be healthy, and detoxify your body. You will be able to eat an unlimited amount of delicious organic vegetables and herbs, as well as some fruits and meats.

The smoothie recipes included are useful in curbing cravings and packing in the nutrients. I figured this out through trial and error. By purchasing this book, you will not have to go through the learning process the same way I did. You can skip ahead to success by using the recipes and implementing them into your new-found Paleolithic lifestyle.

Our ancient ancestors had it right. They did not indulge in processed foods, fast foods and other garbage that is involved in the Neolithic culture of today. Take a blast to the past and find health and wellness in fresh organic foods.

I finally found the one way to be successful in both weight loss and in keeping it off. I know you can do the same using the smoothie recipes in this book in combination with adhering to a Paleo-program! It is easy, fun and delicious. You will never again have to starve yourself in order to shed those excess pounds. Enjoy these scrumptious smoothies while reaching your weight loss goals!

Thanks again for downloading this book, I hope you enjoy it!

Chapter 1 What is Paleo?

Ok, let us get one thing straight at the beginning; the Paleo diet that you have heard everyone raving about and discussing recently is *anything but* a new development in the world of healthy lifestyles and weight loss. The Paleo diet is actually the OLDEST dietary lifestyle that you can adopt. Even though it appears to be the newest, greatest thing "since sliced bread," in reality it is probably the most ancient. Oh, and it has absolutely nothing to do with bread: sliced or unsliced.

The "Paleo diet" is actually a shorter form of the original name for this dietary lifestyle, and yes, it is a *lifestyle*, not a diet at all. The first name coined for this way of eating was actually called the "Paleolithic diet approach." I like the use of the word, "approach." It confirms that this is another way to look at food, shop for food, prepare food, and ingest food. Furthermore, it can be categorized as a lifestyle, a template, or a set of guidelines to live by.

The idea behind this way of looking at food, is to eat as our Paleolithic ancestors once did. The thought is that they were free of modern day ailments and diseases; so it must be best to go back to our roots, to a time when these concerns did not exist. There has to be a correlation between most modern day dietary lifestyles and the high rate of disease, obesity and ailments that plague much of the world today (even more so in western civilization and the US).

Eating paleo is pretty cut and dry once you know the "do's and do not-s." Foods are either included or excluded. Basically the parameters are that you eat nothing that was a development after the rise of agriculture and the use of animal husbandry. This rules out all grain and grain products, legumes, potatoes, beans dairy, sugars, alcohol, and the like. The goal is to consume foods that our hunting, gathering relatives would have eaten.

Foods TO eat are plentiful, especially vegetables and fruits. Lean grass fed meats, some wild caught fish, herbs, raw almonds and pumpkin seeds, herbs and some cold pressed oils are included. There are so many things that you are able to eat, you will not miss the ones you cannot... well not too much anyway.

All of my life I struggled with weight loss and maintenance. I would lose weight, but only for a short time. I would always end up gaining it back, sometimes I would end up gaining more weight than before I had started. It was frustrating and depressing. I would get motivated and excited but end up bored, hungry and disappointed.

I tried everything over the years. Fad diets failed me. Even my favorite, the Grapefruit Diet, sounded like a winner in my quest to drop pounds. I tried pay-for-weight-loss-programs, shelling out hundreds of dollars because the famous people in the commercials were always successful. Needless to say, I never made it far enough on any of these diets to star in the next commercial.

As soon as I heard about the Paleolithic Diet I had to try it. Why? I wanted my body to function optimally while losing weight. It sounded like the most logical eating plan available. I had tried everything illogical, now it was time to try the lifestyle that made the most sense.

My body adapted quickly and I was able to lose weight. Slowly but surely, the pounds melted off. I felt better than I ever had before. Also, because it is more of a lifestyle change than a diet, I was able to keep the weight off for once in my life.

The two things that were most difficult for me were resisting snacking and getting in enough fruits and vegetables every day. One can only eat so many salads bigger than your head. I solved both of these problems with one solution: smoothies. I would use them supplementary every day and they helped me to be successful in losing weight and keeping it off. I have chosen to share my recipes with you so that you might find the same success.

Snacking and cravings are caused by one of two things. The body is either lacking something it needs or it is desiring things it should not have. These smoothies are designed to provide both. They allowed me to get more nutrients into my system on a daily basis, crushing cravings. They also allowed me to make substitutions for old bad habits. By substituting healthy choices for unhealthy ones, I was able to trick my body and get rid of cravings.

I hope that you will use these recipes in conjunction with a Paleo-lifestyle in order to successfully shed excess pounds and keep them off. You do not have to try everything under the sun and experience failure after failure as I did. Even if you have previously been unsuccessful, use the recipes in this book and achieve and even surpass your weight loss goals. It is never too late and you will be so happy and proud of yourself!

Chapter 2 Getting Started

The key to success is in planning and preparation. This chapter will give you a head start in preparing to delve into a Paleo lifestyle. It may appear to be over whelming at the start, but I have tried to break it down in a practical manner so that you can easily jump right in and start finding success in the Paleolithic diet, using smoothies to curb your cravings.

Positivity of the mind is key in being successful in anything, especially when trying to lose weight. I am going to provide you with information and tools that will help you to be informed about the ins and outs of the paleo plan. You will know what you are getting yourself into and will be well prepared for success. This will allow you to start off on the right foot with a positive, "I can do this!" attitude.

Preparation is a key component in being successful at anything, not just being a boy scout, so you will need to make sure that you have the right equipment before you begin. It does not need to be a costly venture; although who can really put a price on wellness and weight loss?

For smoothie making, you will need some kind of blender. Many people already own one, and if you do, the blender that you have will be just fine. Just make sure that it works and you are good to go.

You can, of course buy a pricier, top of the line blender. Vitamix and Blendtec are both top of the line and last forever. There are many other blenders that are a tad less pricey that will still get the job done. Whatever blender you choose will work just fine to prepare delicious paleo smoothies to curb your cravings.

The first thing to do when beginning the paleo diet is to purge your kitchen and pantry of everything you will not be eating. This helps in two ways. One, by following the old adage, "out of sight, out of mind," you will be ridding yourself of things that you cannot have. Two, you will need to make room for all of the fresh, delicious foods that will be the mainstay of your diet.

First of all, you will need to figure out where you will be purchasing your foods. Many supermarkets now carry a variety of organic produce, herbs and grass-fed meats. You can also usually find fresh organic foods at farmer's markets and specialty whole foods stores. To make the most of this lifestyle you will need to buy organic... our ancestors did not have pesticides on their food and neither should you.

I always carry a paleo-acceptable food list with me whenever I shop. You can find many online that are printable. Below I have included most of the foods you will need to purchase in order to eat a paleo diet. There are more detailed lists out there.

1. Fresh organic produce (including seasonal favorites)

   Stay away from starchy vegetables. Limit your fruits, you can get enough of them in your smoothies. Keep your focus on vegetables. Baby spinach, kale, sweet potatoes/yams, cruciferous veggies (broccoli/cauliflower), lettuces/cabbages, peppers, avocado, and mushroom are all staples that you should have on hand most of the time. Add other fun seasonal vegetables when they are available.

2. For protein, organic, hormone-free, grass fed/pasture raised meats are paleo. Do not eat processed or non-organic meats. Wild-caught seafood is also a paleo-friendly option.

3. Animal protein will provide some healthy fats but you will want to keep these items on hand for cooking and supplementation:

   - Organic Extra Virgin Olive Oil

   - Organic Coconut Oil

- Ghee

4. Just because you are eating well does not mean that you have to eat bland. Incorporate organic broths, gluten free dijon mustard, liquid aminos, coconut milk/water, and basically any herb or spice. Raw honey is acceptable as a sweetener, along with pure maple syrup.

5. Tasty fermented food can also be incorporated and are allowable such as: kimchi, kombucha, and sauerkraut. Just make sure that they are non-pasteurized and organic.

6. Additionally you can add these foods in small quantities: raw almonds, cashews, some seeds, pine and Brazil nuts.

You will be eliminating ANYTHING that is processed and should not purchase most things that have ingredients on the label. Vegetables and fresh meats do not have ingredients! Legumes are also prohibited. Beans are also a no-no.

This chapter should help you to get a great start on the Paleolithic lifestyle and all that goes into it. It is simple: stick to produce, wild caught fish and pastured meats. You are now well prepared to dive head on into the only diet that is going to help you lose weight and keep it off by giving your body what it was designed to eat

Chapter 3 Delicious and Healthy Smoothie Recipes

Banana Breakfast

- 1 peeled apple
- 1 banana
- 1 TBS spirulina
- ½ c. kale
- 1 cup coconut water
- ¾ c. ice

1. Peel apple
2. Put all ingredients in blender.
3. Blend well

I love bananas for breakfast. This breakfast smoothie will help you to get your day off in a delicious way. This banana smoothie is perfect for breakfast and incorporates spirulina and kale, helping you to get in some extra nutrients in this morning smoothie. It is an energy boost that will keep you feeling full. You will get fiber, nutrients, and good carbs in one glass!

Spirulina is an excellent supplement to add to many foods or drinks to assist in weight loss. It is high in many nutrients including omega 3s. The body absorbs the protein in spirulina four times better than it does the protein in beef. It is high in nutrients causing your body to signal the brain that you are not hungry.

Berry Blaster

- 1 c. coconut water
- 1 c. each blue, black, and raspberries fresh or frozen (if frozen omit ice)
- 1.5 c. spinach
- 2 TBS raw organic honey
- ¾ c. ice

1. Put all ingredients in blender.
2. Pulse to desired consistency.
3. Enjoy!

Berries, so delicious and so full of nutritional goodness. This is a perfectly sweet and tangy addition to the paleo plan. Enjoy it in the morning for breakfast or in the middle of the day to fulfill that sweet tooth craving. For me, the tanginess is an effective way to curb cravings. The spinach included will also help blast away hunger.

I use coconut water in all of my smoothie recipes because it is super hydrating and it has wonderful flavor. When people get dehydrated one of the first signs is the feeling of hunger. Keep yourself hydrated to prevent snack cravings.

Coconut water is lower on the glycemic index that coconut milk, which is included in many paleo smoothies you will find. The lower the food is on the glycemic index, the less of a spike in your blood sugar levels. This will help with weight loss and help to prevent weight gain as well.

Hunger Hunter

- 1 avocado (peel and pit)

- 1 banana

- 1 c. coconut water

- 1 c. ice

- ¾ c. kale

- ¾ c. spinach

- 2 organic free-range egg yolks*

1. Add all ingredients except for the ice. Blend well.

2. Add ice and pulse until smooth.

3. Enjoy!

This recipe is a sure-fire way to crush cravings and get you through to the next meal. You can use it as a meal replacement or as a snack to get you through to your next meal. It is definitely one of my top five smoothies.

Avocados are full of healthy fats and nutrients. One half contains six grams of fiber. They contain protein, potassium and many vitamins. They keep my stomach full for hours. They are a super fruit. Not to mention they will add a lot of creaminess to any smoothie.

Egg yolks are a great addition to any smoothie on the paleo plan. Make sure they are organic and free-range or pasture raised. The yolks contain protein and omega 3s. They will fill you up and smash your hunger induced cravings.

*Mind you that some "hardcore full-time Paleo extremists" don't eat eggs. But I don't have anything against egg yolks. Enjoy!

Veggie Medley

- ½ bunch kale
- 2 c. collard greens or Swiss chard
- 2 stalks celery
- 1 cucumber
- ½ zucchini
- ½ whole lemon
- 1 green banana
- 1 c. ice

1. Blend all and pulse in ice.
2. Enjoy!

In order to get in enough vegetables to lose weight and be healthy, you can pack them into your day with this yummy, delicious smooth drink. Can you say instant energy?

Vegetables are an essential part of weight loss because they contain all of the vitamins our bodies require to run optimally. If our bodies are not functioning at their finest, we will not lose weight efficiently nor be able to keep excess weight off. In order to enable our bodies to work at one hundred percent we need many minerals and nutrients to support weight loss function.

Iron, calcium, fiber and omega 3s to name a few. All of these are available in large quantities on a paleo diet. One of the best ways to maximize your intake is through supplementing smoothies with a large amount of vegetables and fruits.

Snack Crusher

- 1 TBS melted coconut oil
- 2 organic free-range egg yolks
- 1 banana
- ¾ c. cranberries
- ¾ c. coconut water
- ¾ c. ice

This smoothie will fill you up and you will not feel engorged or weighed down. The cranberry-banana twist will curb your snack craving and help to break the monotony of flavors. Every time I drink this smoothie I feel full for hours on end, essentially ridding myself of the need or want to snack at all.

The liver is able to metabolically breakdown coconut oil fats into energy. It is a medium chain fatty acid, so it is less likely to be stored away as fat on the body.

Cranberries are high in vitamin C, among many other antioxidants. They help the body's conversion of glucose to energy.

Energy in a Glass

- 1 cup broccoli
- 2 c. spinach
- 1 egg yolk
- 1 TBS almond butter
- 1 TBS coconut oil
- 1 oz. pepitas
- 1 cucumber
- 1 ½ c. coconut water
- ½ c. ice

1. Blend all ingredients together except ice.
2. When well blended add the half cup ice and pulse.
3. Enjoy!

Feeling fatigued? This smoothie will be the equivalent of drinking a glass packed with liquid, natural energy. Do not fall off of the Paleo wagon by grabbing a coffee! Mix up a glass of energy and boost yourself without cheating.

Pepitas/pumpkin seeds are paleo-friendly and are great for weight loss. I love them as a snack, but I threw them into one of my favorite smoothies and was hooked. They contain quite a bit of zinc, which is an important because it helps us produce testosterone to burn fat and build muscle. They also have magnesium and iron. Both of these nutrients help the body to remain fatigue-free. Instant energy boost!

Brain Power

- 2 c. blueberries fresh or frozen (if frozen please omit ice)
- 1/2 avocado (pitted and peeled)
- 1c. coconut water
- 1c. ice
- 1 c. spinach or kale

1. Pulse all in blender and enjoy!

When I just can find it in myself to think, I whip up one of these smoothies to instantly lift the brain fog. The blueberries, avocado and spinach are also good for brain health in general. This smoothie helps me to focus on the task at hand without feeling hungry and distracted. It is super delicious as well.

Blueberries have been shown to improve brain function and motor skills. The recommendation is 1 cup/day. Avocado helps to lower blood pressure and allows for healthy blood flow; both of which affect brain function positively.

Pina Cool-ada

- 2c. chilled coconut water
- 1 1/2 c. pineapple (half as much if crushed)
- 2 TBS unrefined coconut oil
- 2 medjool dates (pitted)

1. Put all into blender.
2. Blend well, pulsing often.
3. Enjoy with an umbrella!

Pineapple is rich in fiber, helping to "clean out" wastes and keep you feeling full for longer periods of time. Bromelain is an enzyme in pineapples that breaks down both fat and protein. Bromelain also aids in cleaning out your digestive system. It contains B vitamins that convert carbs into energy, so boost your motivation with refreshing pineapple.

Berry Nice

- 1 c. each blue, black, and raspberries frozen or fresh (if frozen omit ice)

- 1c. ice

- 1 ½ c. coconut water

- ½ banana

- 2 c. spinach

1. Blend all, pulsing often because of frozen berries/ice.
2. Enjoy!

I love berries. I cannot say enough good things about them. They are amazing, and where I live you can get them fresh all year. If this is not the case in your region, or you just prefer to use frozen berries, please do. The spinach will add a nice background flavor, and when serving to children it is an easy way to get in some undetected veggies.

Blackberries contain more antioxidants than all of the other fruits in the paleo plan. They have a high fiber content that will keep you feeling full for hours.

Raspberries are very low on the glycemic index, so they are a great way to get in some sweetness while keeping the blood sugar levels even. They are also high in fiber; fill up on delicious berries for weight loss.

Glass is Greener

- 1 1/2 c. coconut water
- 4 celery stalks
- ½ lemon
- 4 each Kale and romaine leaves
- 1 c. spinach
- ½ apple
- ½ cucumber
- ½ bell pepper
- 1 c. ice

1. Core apple and mix all in blender.
2. Pulse in ice.

This is by far my favorite "classic" green smoothie. It incorporates so many different green vegetables and does not leave a bad taste in your mouth. Share this recipe with friends when they ask for one of those "popular green drinks."

Celery and cucumber both have a high water content. They are perfect vegetables for hydrating the body, and we all know how important hydration is for weight loss and maintenance. These two veggies in combination with coconut water will set you up for a super dose of hydration.

Smooth Sailin'

- 1 Papaya
- 1 kiwi
- 1 c. broccoli florets
- 1 pitted peach
- 1c. coconut water
- 1 c. ice

1. Pulse all in blender and enjoy!

Feeling constipated? Well you should not often, being that you are eating a lot of vegetables, but every now and again it happens to the best of us. Constipation will leave you feeling fat and bloated. It will also stop you from eliminating the wastes you want to get rid of in order to lose weight this smoothie tackles this problem head on.

Papaya is not only great for elimination (which of course aids in weight loss), it contains papain. Papain is an enzyme that helps the body to break up protein leading to weight loss.

Mango Madness

- 2 mango
- ½ banana
- 2 c. spinach
- 2 TBS raw honey
- 1 c. ice

1. Peel and slice mango (If using frozen, use about 1-1/2 c. and no ice).
2. Add all ingredients to blender and blend well.
3. Pour and enjoy!

Mango is addicting. There, I said it, I have a problem. I can eat 50 at a time without breaking a sweat. This is not a good thing. I came up with this smoothie recipe to help ensure that I would not go overboard, yet would get to have my mango fix.

This smoothie is useful in a paleo weight loss lifestyle for two reasons, it is packed with fiber and contains honey. Raw honey is low on the glycemic index. It is also high in nutrients, something that other sugars are not.

Date Deliciousness

- 1/3 c. pitted medjool dates
- 1c. coconut water
- 1 c. ice
- ½ pitted and peeled avocado
- ¼ teaspoon cinnamon
- Put all of the ingredients into blender and pulse.

This is one smoothie that I turn to when I am craving sweets. It is so scrumptious and will quickly distract your mind from ingesting a bunch of brownies or cookies. I find myself craving these sweets in the afternoon on occasion, and when I do, you better believe I whip up one of these. The medjool date is a superb replacement for desert in the paleo lifestyle!

The cinnamon in this smoothie helps to regulate blood sugar and insulin levels in the body. It helps to prevent fat storage through this insulin-regulation and also helps metabolize sugars. In addition, cinnamon helps keep food in your stomach longer before it moves on to your intestines, making you feel full for a longer period of time. Lastly, cinnamon helps your body to process carbs. What an amazing little spice.

Fruit-o-pia

- ½ green banana
- ½ green apple
- ½ c. each blueberries and blackberries
- 1 c. watermelon
- ½ lemon (peeled)
- 1 c. coconut water
- ½ c. ice

1. Put all into blender, mixing well.
2. Pulse in ice.

Sometimes our bodies crave things that we need, and on occasion people mistake a deficiency of vitamins for a sweet tooth. Pack in the sweet fruits and the vitamins of this smoothie when craving a desert. You will get vitamins, healthy sugars, and hydration, all in one low calorie glass of fruit utopia.

Vegetable Desire

- 1 c. each: collard greens, Swiss chard, spinach
- 2 celery stalks
- 1/2 c. each cauliflower and broccoli florets
- 1 cucumber
- ¼ onion
- 1 handful dandelion greens
- 2 medjool dates
- 1 cup coconut water
- ½ c. ice

1. Blend up all ingredients except for ice.
2. Pulse in ice.
3. Pour and enjoy.

After I had been paleo for a few months, I craved raw veggies constantly. My entire system was reprogrammed. My body would signal me if I had not eaten enough that day or the day before. I was addicted. When I felt that lacking of nutrients from deep within one day, I came up with this recipe to get my fix. I love it and every paleo I have shared it with has come to agree with me. It is one of my best tools in my weight loss arsenal.

Veggie-a-Go-Go

- 3 c. spinach

- 1 ½ cups coconut water

- ½ c. ice

- 1 peeled lime

- 1 cucumber

1. Blend all and enjoy!

If you need an energy boost to get you motivated for a workout, a trip to the energy drink aisle is a waste of your life and your time. Make up one of these smoothies in the same amount of time it would take you to make a pot of coffee or drive to get an energy drink.

Caliente Verde Veggie

- 1 bunch kale
- ½ lime
- ½ bunch cilantro
- 2 stalks celery
- 1/8 teaspoon cayenne pepper
- 1 c. filtered water
- 1 c. ice

1. Blend all and enjoy!

I love spicy foods. I figured why not make a spicy smoothie and drink it? I love this drink in the morning. It really wakes up the whole body. It is mean and green and possibly in my top 5 favorite smoothies.

Cayenne pepper will help speed up your weight loss. Cayenne increases metabolism by up to 25 percent. Capsaicin is the responsible chemical in fat loss. It activates a protein in your body that helps to prevent the development of fat.

Simply Smooth

- 1 avocado (peel and pit)
- ¼ c. coconut milk
- 1 c. coconut water
- ½ c. ice
- 1 cucumber

1. Blend all except the ice for as long as possible.
2. Pulse in ice, or omit ice and freeze for ½ hour.
3. Enjoy!

This recipe was invented for a dear friend who has a problem... she loves ice creams and puddings. She wanted a smooth smoothie. I used a tiny bit of coconut milk in this recipe and you will notice I do not do that often as it is much more sugary than coconut water. She loves this smoothie and to be honest, so do I!

Motivational Mango

- 1 frozen mango
- 1 cup ice
- 1 cup coconut water
- 2 cups spinach

1. Blend all in a blender.
2. Enjoy the fruit of your labor!

Yes there is another recipe dedicated to my favorite tropical fruit and edible love interest: the mango. I just cannot get enough of it. A few months ago I decided that I needed more variety in my mango addiction and came up with this. It helps to curb my cravings for sweet, delectable treats. It also keeps my full-blown addiction under control and prevents mango overdose. Summertime in a glass, even in the middle of winter (use frozen mango).

Guava Goodness

- 1 cup of guava
- 2 cups spinach
- ¼ lemon peeled
- 1 teaspoon grated ginger
- ½ cup papaya
- 1 cup coconut water
- 1 cup ice

1. Put all ingredients into blender and mix to desired consistency.
2. Pulse in ice.
3. Enjoy!

This tropical smoothie will give you a little bit of indulgence in the middle of a chaotic day. Take a deep breath and a break with this fruity and fabulous smoothie. It also makes a good substitute for a blended alcoholic beverage. Just throw in an umbrella and indulge without slacking off on your weight loss journey!

Ginger helps with the digestive processes in the body. It is also a fat burner. Lastly it helps you to feel fuller for longer periods of time, this will reduce the amount of fat and calories that you ingest every day.

Cucumber Cooler

- 2 cucumbers
- 1 celery stalk
- ½ avocado (peel and pit)
- ¼ bunch cilantro
- 1 cup coconut water
- ½ cup ice

1. Blend all and refresh!

Cucumber is ultra-refreshing. On a hot day, nothing beats the taste and goodness of a cold cucumber. People put them on their eyes for goodness sake, why not make a cucumber smoothie and refresh from the inside out?

Cilantro naturally works as a diuretic for the body. It also contains limonene. Limonene may help to reduce or keep belly fat from forming. It can also reduce bloating within twenty four hours.

Zucchini Zip

- 1 zucchini
- ½ green apple
- ¼ teaspoon cinnamon
- 1 cup spinach
- 1 cup coconut water
- ½ c. ice

1. Blend all ingredients.
2. Pulse ice and enjoy!

I love zucchini and adore the spice that cinnamon adds to it. It is a beautiful flavor combination that is further enhanced with the apple. This is one of my favorite morning smoothies and I have been known to drink it in place of breakfast (you can add an egg yolk or two if desired and it will not alter the taste too much).

Zucchini is great for weight loss. It contains few calories and is packed with vitamins and flavonoids. You can eat a ton of it without eating a bunch of calories.

Watermelon Wasted

- 2½ cups chopped watermelon

- 1 cup strawberries (fresh or frozen)

- 1 cup broccoli florets

- ½ c. spinach

- ½ cup coconut water

- ½ cup ice (you can omit if using frozen berries)

1. Put all in blender and mix to desired consistency.

2. Enjoy!

Watermelon is great as an alkalizing agent and it is full of water. It will help to hydrate your body and has a flavor like no other fruit. Young and old seem to appreciate the flavors in this smoothie as they are pretty unique.

Watermelon is an excellent food for weight loss. It is low calorie, hydrating and packed with nutrients. If you are working out, add the white part of the melon to your smoothie. The white part is an amino acid called citrulline and is useful in muscle recovery.

Mediterranean Gazpacho Smoothness

- 2 TBS sliced green onion
- 2 TBS chopped white ground pepper
- 2 TBS lemon juice
- ¼ chopped celery
- ½ cup peeled and chopped cucumber
- ¼ cup shredded carrot
- 1 ½ cups peeled, diced and seeded tomatoes
- ½ cup plain yogurt
- ½ TBS ground black pepper
- ½ TBS extra virgin olive oil
- 4 basil leaves
- 1 small clove of garlic

1. Put all ingredients except basil leaves in blender and mix well
2. Cool the gazpacho in the fridge for at least half an hour
3. Serve chilled in a bowl, decorated with basil leaves
4. Enjoy!

Gazpacho is one of my favorite dinner-time paleo smoothies. Not only can it fill your stomach for hours and give you the necessary energy and healthy fats you need (olive oil), but also tastes out of this earth. I fell in love with gazpachos at first tablespoon when I was visiting my Spanish friends in Barcelona during my summer vacation. Spaniards drink it every day to renew their strength during fiery hot summer days. You should definitely try that one! Healthy, nutritious and just   simply   delicious!

Celery Citrus Snack

- 2 celery stalks
- 1/3 cucumber
- Handful of spinach
- ½ lemon peeled
- 1 cup coconut water
- ½ cup ice
- 3 mint leaves

1. Put all ingredients in blender and mix well.
2. Enjoy!

This hydrating smoothie is one of my favorites for warm weather. Its hydrating qualities prevent snacking. The mint and citrus twist add an interesting flavor combination to the same vegetables that are used in most paleo smoothies.

Mint is good for weight loss. Something about the taste suppresses appetite. Throw it in a smoothie and you will have added appetite suppression.

Kale Kup

- 1 bunch kale
- 1 cup coconut water
- ½ cup ice
- 1 TBSP coconut oil
- 1 green banana

1. Mix all in a blender.
2. Pour in your kup and enjoy!

Kale is one of my favorite vegetables in the paleo plan. It is nutrient dense and leaves me feeling full for hours on end. You get a whole bunch of kale in one smoothie and it tastes fabulous.

Kale is a fabulous weight loss food because not only is it high in fiber to clean you out and help you feel full, it is packed with phytonutrients, tons of vitamins and minerals. It is a super food and a sure fire way to make sure you get a lot of it into your system every day is by supplementing what you eat with what you drink.

1 green banana will increase your metabolism, which is excellent for weight loss. It contains 12.5 gr. of resistant starches. RS are converted into short chained fatty acids in the intestine. Green banana goodness.

Red Bliss

- ½ large raw beetroot, grated
- 1/3 avocado
- handful of blueberries
- TBSP dried berries (you can use cranberries as a substitute)
- TBSP linseed meal
- 3 big strawberries (or more smaller ones)
- 1 teaspoon organic palm oil
- ½ tsp yacon powder (or lucuma)
- ½ cup coconut milk
- coconut water

1. Mix all in a blender.
2. Eat with spoon. If you want to drink it, add more coconut water or ice.

You should know that beetroot is one of my favorite veggies. Why is that?

Not only the taste plays the role here. Beetroots work toning for the liver, purify the blood, help in reducing the pressure and remove uric acid from the body. Consumption of sugar provides maximum detoxification of your body.

Also, helps to nitrates, beetroot helps you exercise better. It slows down the absorption of the oxygen, and so it helps you endure more and tire much slower.

Happy Baobab Smoothie

- ½ teaspoon baobab fruit powder
- ½teaspoon yacon powder / lucuma
- 1 cup fresh strawberries with a generous squeeze of lemon juice
- 1/3 avocado
- 1 teaspoon of Tahini

1. Put all ingredients in blender and mix well
2. This smoothie is very rich and if you want to drink it, it needs some additional coconut water as well.
3. Enjoy!

Baobab fruit powder is a powerful vitamin bomb. Baobab fruits contain 6 times more antioxidants than blueberries, 6 times more vitamin C than oranges, 6 times more potassium than bananas and 2 times more calcium than milk. It supports the digestive system- the powder is rich in digestive enzymes and probiotics, which increase the growth of bacteria needed in the digestive tract. It optimizes the absorption of iron. And of course, thanks to fiber, it helps you lost weight, and then maintain it.

Tahini makes this smoothie even healthier and more nutritious - sesame seeds provide the body with valuable nutrients, are a source of protein, magnesium, vitamin B12, healthy fat, calcium required for blood vessels, carbohydrates, amino acids, antioxidants (sesamol and sesamolina) – all this causes human cells to age more slowly.

Coconut Song

- 1 cup full fat coconut milk, chilled
- 1 cup ice
- 2 large fresh peaches, peeled and cut
- fresh lime zest
- 1 fresh pineapple ring

1. Add coconut milk, ice and peaches to blender. Use a rasper to add a few gratings of fresh lime zest. Additionally, you can add a squeeze of fresh lime juice.
2. Blend until everything goes smooth

The tropical subtle taste of coconut makes me want to sing almost every time I drink it (preferably "She put de lime in de coconut, she drank dem bot up! ")
In Sanskrit, the coconut palm is known under the name "kalpa vriksha", which means "tree that provides everything needed for life".

Coconut flesh has strong antibacterial, antiviral and antifungal properties, treats diseases of the digestive tract (diarrhea, vomiting, intoxication) and hydrates the body complementing the level of electrolytes.

Although this drink is totally delicious and so healthy, don't drink it too often as fat coconut milk is very nourishing and satiating, and too large amount of it could subtract from your energy. I drink this smoothie no more than 2-3 times a week. Don't forget to sing the song after you do!

Cherry-na-na Tango

- 1 cup frozen unsweetened cherries
- ½ ripe banana
- ½ cup coconut milk
- ½ teaspoon organic raw honey
- 1 teaspoon flaxseed meal
- 5 ice cubes

1. Put all ingredients in blender and mix well.
2. Enjoy!

I love the dance of both banana and cherry taste on my tongue. Flaxseed meal will make you feel full for a long time, and the honey will add even more to this wonderful deliciousness. This smoothie makes a perfect mixture to start your day with!

Vigorous Choco Delicacy

- 1 cup raw almond milk (without sugar)
- 6 pitted medjool dates
- Split ice-cold banana
- 1-2 TBSP organic cocoa powder or few organic dark chocolate cubes (70%-90% is the best)

1. Put the almond milk, the dates and cocoa/chocolate in a blender first. Mix well. Add the banana, and blend again until everything is perfectly smooth.
2. Serve promptly.
3. You may want to add or substract from the cocoa, just adjust it to your own taste.

I've got this recipe from my Moroccan friend when I was travelling in North Africa. You may be wondering- is cocoa a bean or a legume? No! They're pod seeds and they're extremely healthy!

Cocoa is considered to be a rich source of antioxidants such as procyanidins and flavanoids, which may impart anti aging properties. It helps keeping low rate of heart disease and cancer and improves blood flow. It regenerates the body after exercise, both physically and mentally. It also significantly improves the functioning of the brain and memory. Also, dates in this drink will give your body enough energy and keep it from food cravings for good few hours. And it's totally delicious. The taste of almond goes perfectly with cocoa and dates giving the smoothie the unique oriental taste.

The Smashing Pumpkin

- 1 cup unsweetened almond milk
- ½ cup frozen raspberries
- A handful of cashew nuts
- ¼ teaspoon fresh ginger
- teaspoon of ground cloves
- ½ cup smashed pumpkin

1. Put all ingredients in blender and mix well.

2. Add ginger

3. Enjoy!

This is an old recipe I've got from my beloved grandmother and modified a little bit.

Mind you that especially valuable is the pumpkin with orange flesh, as it contains a lot of carotene (provitamin A) - the more intense the color of the flesh, the more vitamins it has in it. Pumpkin Fruit recommended to people with atherosclerosis, arteriosclerosis, hypertension, and also in cases of renal insufficiency edema, heart or liver. Just one handful of cashew nuts supplies our body with the very best: healthy fat, protein, carbohydrates, fiber, magnesium, phosphorus, iron, zinc and starch, vitamin A, E and PP. Ginger speeds up your metabolism, helps digestion and increases thermo genesis which helps weight loss.

Frozen raspberries, ground cloves and fresh ginger will give this smoothie very fresh, unique and enticing taste. I felt in love with it so many years ago!

This smoothie is indeed a real smashing healthy combo!

Delectable Wakame Fatburner

- 2 TBSP Wakame edible seaweed (fresh and not salt-conserved)
- ¼ teaspoon black ground pepper
- 2 TBSP organic maple syrup
- 1 cup frozen strawberries
- 1 cup frozen cherries
- 1 teaspoon organic honey
- ½ cup ice

1. Pour Wakame seaweed with cold water, leave it for 10-15 minutes (at this time it will significantly increase its volume, so it's best to put them in a bowl). Leave to drain in a strainer.

2. Put all ingredients in blender and mix well.

3. Enjoy!

Wakame is widely used in Asian cuisine (e.g. soups and salad dressings).

This wonderful seaweed contains a balanced combination of basic organic minerals, including iron, calcium, magnesium, and valuable elements. Additionally, Wakame is known for its detoxifying antioxidants, Omega 3 fatty acids (in the form of eicosapentaenoic acid) and as a good source of vegetable proteins. Wakame also provides a variety of vitamins such as vitamin C and B, and serves as an excellent source of both soluble and insoluble fiber. Not only is Wakame healthy, but also contains Fucoxanthin which recently proved to be a great fat burner.

Tropical Green

- 2 cups fresh kale
- 1 cup of coconut milk
- 1 cup of cubed pineapple
- 1 whole mango, peeled and frozen
- 1 whole kiwi fruit, peeled and diced
- Juice of ½ lime

1. Peel the mango and freeze it. Peel and cube kiwi fruit and pineapple.
2. Put mango, kiwi, kale, pineapple, lime juice and coconut milk in blender.
3. Blend nicely. Enjoy chilled with ice cubes.

This is definitely one of my most favorite vegetable-fruit smoothies, not only because it contains my favorite mango but because every ingredient present in this smoothie is completely natural and doesn't add on to weight gain issue considerably. Mango is in fact considered as a good fruit option for people like me who are trying to lose weight. This is because mangoes are low energy density food options and therefore, replacing it with high energy density food options makes me put on less weight while staying full and active.

Berry Best

- 1 cup of coconut water (use chilled if desired)
- 1 cup of blackberry
- 2 cups of strawberry
- 2 cups of blueberry
- 1 cup of raspberry
- A dash of honey
- Ice cubes

1. Tip all the berries in the blender along with coconut water and a dash of honey.
2. Blend well to combine
3. Pour in a tall glass, chill out the smoothie with ice cubes.

This smoothie is a wonder in itself. Who would not love a glass of smoothie prepared from a bunch of berries? I love this smoothie and so does my paleo diet. The fibers from these amazingly nutritious fruits keep from full, while providing me with the essential supplements like vitamin C. I also love how simple it is to prepare and how everybody in my house relishes it. Paleo, nutritious and weight managing. This smoothie is a perfect example of beauty with brain and I will never give up loading tons of it in my stomach.

Watermelon Berry Slurpee

- 1 cup of watermelon, cubed, seeded and chilled
- 2 strawberries
- 6-8 blueberries
- ½ cup of coconut water
- ½ guava
- Ice cubes

1. Cube the watermelon and chill it.
2. Tip watermelon cubes, berries, ½ of a guava and coconut water into a blender.
3. Blend until thoroughly combined and smooth.
4. Toss in ice cubes and enjoy.

This is probably the most unique fruit smoothie combination I have ever come across. Guava with watermelon and berries is a killer combination and it is a treat to paleo eaters. This smoothie is an example of how one can be free to experiment with paleo food and never give up on this eating tendency. It is definitely one of my favorites. Other than being super delicious and taste buds friendly, ingredients used in this smoothie also promote weight loss, as guava and watermelon provides the essential amount of fiber and the huge water content in watermelon helps keep the stomach full for a longer time, thereby curbing food cravings.

Papaya Surprise

- 1 small papaya, peeled, seeded and cubed
- 4-6 tablespoons of pure honey
- 1 whole ripe banana, peeled and halved
- ½ cup of coconut milk
- 4 tablespoons of raspberries
- 2-3 strawberries

1. Fill up a blender with the strawberries, raspberries, papaya cubes and banana. Add the honey and coconut milk.
2. Blend until smooth and no more lumpy in texture.
3. Toss in a few ice cubes and serve chilled.

Papaya is one of the best fruits to have while trying to reduce weight. Not only because it has fiber to substitute for calorie rich food but because papaya also has digestion promoting properties. Papaya can effectively help reduce bloating and other digestion problems. This in turn helps to keep the body fit, thereby boosting the body's capability to keep up with regular exercising and weight loss programs. Apart from papaya, banana present in this smoothie supplements for meal and provide the essential calories. This is a wonderfully filling and comforting paleo smoothie recipe which also amazingly reduces weight.

Green Coconut

- 1 whole banana, peeled and sliced
- 2 cups of kale
- 1 large carrot
- 1 tablespoon of honey
- 1 cup of coconut milk
- 1 half tomato

1. Halve the tomato and slice the banana and carrot.
2. Tip the coconut milk and fruits into the blender. Blend.
3. Add the kale at last and blend for 30 seconds or until smooth.
4. Enjoy chilled with ice cubes.

This is one of those vegetable smoothies which haven never repulsed me. The banana and the honey makes up for the bitterness of the vegetables and makes this a great and nutritious vegetable smoothies for people trying to lose weight. This smoothie is a great replacement for solid food and meals and thus promotes weight loss. To top that, this wonderful smoothie is also a great source of vitamin K, B1, A, B6 and C, making it a win-win situation for the people like me trying to lose weight.

Creamy Peach

- 1 cup of coconut milk
- 1 whole fresh peach, sliced
- 1 whole banana, peeled and sliced
- 1 teaspoon of fresh lemon juice
- Ice cubes

1. Peel and slice the banana and the peach.
2. Add the peach and banana into the blender after the coconut milk and lemon juice.
3. Blend until creamy and smooth.
4. Drop in ice cubes and enjoy the creamy smoothie chilled.

Peaches are one of those summer fruits I never get tired of eating. Peaches are even wonderful for weight loss as these super delicious fruits are rich in calories high enough to suffice up for the high calorie meals. A 6 ounce sized peach can provide as much as 68 calories, making it a great resort for people trying to check their weight. Moreover, the high water content in peach and in this smoothie as a whole helps to keep the stomach feeling full, thereby curbing hunger. However; the trick to indulge in this fruit while still reducing weight is to have it in moderation and pairing it with a low calorie diet. This creamy smoothie is awesome for hot summer days and can be consumed the every other day.

- 1 whole banana, peeled and sliced
- 2 cups of chilled coconut milk
- 1 teaspoon of crushed almonds
- 8-10 fresh large leaves spinach
- 7-8 leaves kale

1. Blend banana with coconut milk.
2. Blend in the kale and spinach and stir in the crushed almond.
3. Toss in some ice cubes and serve chilled.

Kale is one of the best veggies to have while being on paleo diet and trying to reduce weight. Packed with vitamin A, nutrients, fiber and antioxidants, kale is termed as one of the best vegetables to have for weight loss. Since kale is super bitter vegetable, I find it best to consume in the form of a smoothie. This smoothie is one of the best kale smoothies, as it contains almonds and the almonds provide this smoothie the required calorie to promote weight loss in a healthy way. I never feel like I am drinking a vegetable smoothie with this one and I strongly recommend it for weight loss program on paleo diet.

Minty Strawberry

- 6-8 fresh strawberries
- A handful of fresh mint leaves
- 1 glass of chilled water
- 1/2 teaspoon of honey

1. Blend the strawberries with mint leaves in water.
2. Blend in the honey and serve chilled with ice cubes.

What can be more refreshing than a smoothie made of strawberries and mint? This is a weight checker's dream smoothie, at least it's mine. I just can't think of a hot day without it. A completely paleo and weight loss boosting smoothie, this smoothie keeps me full for a long time. This is one of the best smoothies to have even after an exercise session and even when I sometimes feel lethargic to continue with exercises on a hot summer day. Low on fat and nutrient rich, the minty strawberry smoothie is a must have for me.

Orange Splash

- 1 whole orange, peeled and sliced
- 1 teaspoon of honey
- ½ banana, peeled and sliced
- 2 fresh strawberries, stemmed
- 1 glass of coconut water
- A handful of chopped pineapple

1. Peel and slice the banana and pineapple.
2. Blend the fruits with the coconut water until smooth.
3. Drop a few ice cubes in the glass and serve right away.

The bunch of different types of fruits present in this smoothie always makes me want more of it. Being a completely fruit smoothie, this one helps me counter weight gain and also keeps me full. From the pineapple to strawberries, every fruit present in this concoction helps fight excess body fat and the vitamins and nutrients present on the juice keeps me fit and active, thus promoting weight loss.

This is a perfect smoothie for curbing cravings. The low glycemic index of coconut water is excellent for people trying to lose weight, as this helps in keeping the hunger pangs at bay for a long time by keeping the body hydrated and the stomach full for a long time. Coconut water has been used in this smoothie instead of coconut milk to make it low on calorie level, yet very strategically increasing the fiber level.

Creamy Spinach Salsa

- 1 cup of fresh spinach leaves
- 1 whole avocado, pitted, peeled and diced
- 1 teaspoon of fresh lemon juice
- 1 cup of water

1. Peel and dice the avocado.
2. Blend the avocado with water and then add the spinach
3. Blend until smooth. Add the lemon juice. Blend again.
4. Serve as it is or chilled with ice cubes.

Spinach, avocado and lemon juice is a unique combination. Although it is not a treat to the taste buds, nor do I enjoy drinking it every time, I simply love how the avocado and lemon juice beats the flavor of spinach and makes this smoothie worth of drinking. I indulge in this smoothie quite often due to the fact that spinach is a great source of fiber and a single glass of this amazing smoothie keeps me away from calorie rich food for the entire day. Moreover, it is a super low calorie and the lemon juice present in this smoothie also promotes weight loss.

Cherish Celery

- 8-10 fresh maraschino cherries
- ½ cup of celery head
- 1 tablespoon of honey
- 1 cup of chilled coconut milk

1. Stem the maraschino cherries and tip those into a blender.
2. Add the coconut milk and blend.
3. Add the celery heads and honey and blend again until smooth.
4. Serve chilled with ice cubes.

Can you believe that celery can be a cool food and it can be cherished in a smoothie? At least I couldn't until I tasted this smoothie myself. I was really skeptical about its taste the first time I was about to try it. However; the slight sweet taste of honey and maraschino cherries present in this smoothie has made it the best celery smoothie I have ever had. I now enjoy this mix quite often and it is simply a pleasure for me to know how the celery, honey and cherries help promote weight loss. I never knew but celery is termed as a "miracle" vegetable for weight loss. It's also is a good source of carbohydrate with almost zero fat in it and therefore the best vegetable to have whenever I feel hungry and crave food. Apart from keeping me full for a longer time, this smoothie also provides me with most of the essential nutrients and vitamins like vitamin A, potassium, vitamin K2 and Vitamin B 6.

Pine Fruit Tree

- 5-6 pineapple cubes
- 1 whole apple, peeled and seeded
- A handful of fresh grapes
- 1 whole banana, peeled
- 4 strawberries
- 1 kiwi fruit
- ½ cup of watermelon cubes, seeded
- 1 cup of coconut milk

1. Peel the banana, pineapple and apple.
2. Blend all the fruits one by one with coconut milk.
3. Blends until everything is well mixed.
4. Serve with ice cubes and enjoy.

Continuing a weight loss program, especially on the Paleo diet, seemed like a very much impossible task for me when I started. However; I drank this smoothie for the first time and it just blew off my mind. I was simply stunned and very much convinced this time that this smoothie is my way to go. This was one of the very first smoothies I tried for weight loss ever since I decided to be on the paleo diet. I strongly recommend this particular smoothie to every person who dread aspiring a weight loss plan while being paleo, as the apple has enough fiber to put me at ease even when I no longer indulge in gluteneous foods and the calorie count found in banana helps me keep going without feeling hunger pangs even after working out.

Yellow Flames

- 1 whole banana
- ½ cup of pumpkin, cubed
- ½ cup of squash, cubed
- 1 cup of coconut milk
- 1 teaspoon of honey

1. Blend the banana with coconut milk.
2. Add in squash and pumpkin and blend until smooth.
3. Add in honey and serve.

A beautiful, filing smoothie for every weight controller, yellow flames is one of those smoothies which will keep you motivated for your weight loss program, at least it does so for me. I am a very bad weight controller myself and always gorged on food even I felt full. However; I no longer feel anything like that ever since I started treating me with this smoothie. A gorgeous combination of pumpkin, squash, banana and honey, this smoothie is unbelievably good for weight loss, yet practically potential for the same. All of the three fruits are loaded with fibers and when taken in moderation, this smoothie not only promotes weight loss by fighting fatty cells but also keeps the mind and body refreshing and fit to boost the weight loss program.

Red Sea

- 1 whole beetroot
- 1 whole carrot
- 1 cup of pomegranate
- 1 cup of seeded watermelon, cubed
- 1 cup of coconut water

1. Blend the pomegranate and watermelon with coconut water.
2. Blend the turnip and carrot until smooth.
3. Serve cool or chilled.

I love this smoothie right from its name. It's just so impossible to resist and I simply can't do without this smoothie at least once in one or two weeks. It's all the goodness in one smoothie. Rich in beta carotene, this smoothie keeps me fight my weight loss challenge, without even making me feel deprived. Beet roots being low on calorie density helps suffice up for the calorie, without adding on to the fat levels. Apart from that, beet root is also known to reduce the levels of triglycerides and HDL from the blood, thereby fighting off bad cholesterol and giving way to weight loss promotion. Additionally, beet roots, carrots and watermelons being rich in fibers, keep digestive problems at bay and giving way to faster

Fruit and Nuts

- 10-12 fresh strawberries
- ½ cup of almonds, crushed
- 1 cup of coconut milk
- 1 whole banana
- 1 teaspoon of lime juice

1. Peel and slice the banana.
2. Blend the banana slices and strawberries with coconut milk.
3. Add in the crushed almonds and lime juice and blend.
4. Serve once ready.

A perfect combination, fruits and nuts smoothie is one of my favorites. The nutty flavor of this smoothie will surely blow of your mind and will never make you feel that you are on a weight loss program.

Consuming a whole lot of fruits and nuts are essential for effective and fast weight loss. While nuts are pretty high on calorie content, the cholesterol content of nuts is mostly based on LDL instead of HDL. Rather, this LDL content helps fight off the HDL and triglyceride content on blood, thereby giving way to faster weight loss. This smoothie is therefore one of the best smoothies to have before workouts as the energy content of the nuts will keep you going longer while working out.

Apart from the nuts, the fruits present in this smoothie are rich sources of vitamins, minerals, antioxidants and fibers. These things keep me active and fit and the high water content of these fruits keep my body well hydrated even when working out.

Tomato Tango

- 1 cup of tomato cubes
- ½ teaspoon of lemon juice
- 1 carrot
- 1 whole cucumber
- ½ cup of water

1. Cut the vegetables into small cubes.
2. Blend the vegetables with water. Finish with lemon juice.
3. Serve the refreshing smoothie chilled.

I don't really think that this smoothie needs any introduction as a promoter of weight loss, considering the ingredients list. Tomato is termed as a must have food for weight loss. Studies suggest that consuming tomatoes on a daily basis can help a person lose weight in just 15 days. Moreover, it's tasty as well. Hence, as I was super excited to get acquainted about the tremendous potentiality of tomato for weight loss, I immediately decided to give this smoothie a try and today it is yet another favorite smoothies of mine.

Tomatoes and carrots being rich in antioxidants, helps promote weight loss by boosting the immune system and metabolism. Other than that, tomato is also known to reverse leptin resistance, a phenomenon which regulates the metabolism and promotes faster weight loss. Being high on water content, this smoothie keeps the stomach full for a longer duration while maintaining a balanced blood sugar level.

Flower Garden

- ½ cup of chopped cauliflower
- 1 tomato
- ½ cup of broccoli florets
- 1 cup of spinach
- 1 teaspoon of fresh lemon juice
- 1 cup of chilled water
- Ice cubes

1. Chop broccoli florets and cauliflower florets into small pieces.
2. Blend broccoli with cauliflower, tomato, spinach, water and lemon juice.
3. Serve chilled and enjoy.

Having a veggie smoothie is your best bet if you are trying to put a stop on your weight gaining spree. This veggie smoothie here is one of the extremely potent weight loss veggie smoothies as it contains both spinach and broccoli. Both spinach, broccoli and cauliflower are fiber rich and promote easy weight loss by normalizing the digestive system and purifying the body to excrete the excess fat. Apart from that, cauliflower is also known to reduce water retention in the body, thereby keeping bloating and other digestive disorders at bay. A perfect after-workout smoothie, but also ideal for lunch and dinner. The vegetables present in this one are extremely filling, which keep the body feeling full without adding on to the fat content. Apart from the green vegetables, tomato acts as a brownie point by boosting the metabolism, relieving water retention and boating and by keeping the body hydrated all day long. So, if you are on paleo diet and are trying to lose some pounds, do give this awesome smoothie a try.

Blue Ocean

- 1 cup of blueberries
- 1 cup of blackberries
- 4 strawberries
- 1 cup of water
- A dash of honey

1. Blend the berries with water in blender.
2. Add the honey and blend until no longer lumpy.
3. Serve chilled with ice cubes.

Ummmm, my absolute favorite! Blue Ocean is one such smoothie that I simply can't stop thinking about and gorging on. I love this smoothie not only because of its taste and because it is weight loss promoting smoothie but also because it is probably one of the easiest to prepare. You just throw the fruits in the blender and blend it all together to prepare yourself a cool and refreshing smoothie.

The reason that berries are considered good for weight loss is that these fruits are extremely rich in antioxidants and because these are also extremely low on calorie content. So, make sure you make yourself a gorgeous smoothie like this on a regular basis and make weight loss a delight for yourself.

Nutty Apple

- 1 large apple
- A handful of walnuts
- A dash of lemon juice
- 8-10 grapes
- 1 cup of coconut milk

1. Blend the apple and grapes with coconut milk.
2. Add lemon juice and walnuts. Blend again for a few minutes until well combined.
3. Serve in glasses and enjoy.

Loaded with vitamin, minerals and of course fiber, apples are termed as the king of fruits in terms of health benefits. While you may be aware of various health benefits of apples, the fact that apples can draw cholesterol out of the blood stream is simply a stunner. Fibers present in apples get mixed with bile on coming in contact with water and forms a gelatinous substance, which eventually draws cholesterol out of the blood stream. Apart from that, apples also help reduce appetite by getting swelled up in the stomach.

Figs and Fruits

- 2 whole figs
- ½ cup of watermelon
- 1 peach
- 1 banana
- 2 seeded dates
- ½ orange
- 1 cup of coconut water

1. Seed the dates and throw into blender.
2. Blend the fruits with the dates and coconut water.
3. Blend until everything is combined.
4. Serve with ice cubes.

Figs and Fruits is one of such smoothies that you can indulge in occasionally. However, it is undoubtedly better than gorging on high calorie foods. 1 large fig is equivalent to 47 calories, which is lesser than high calorie foods but it's sufficient enough to curb the hunger pangs. This awesome smoothie can be consumed anytime during the day and dealt with the sweet cravings. Apart from that the other fruits like banana also make this smoothie a highly comforting and filling smoothie and thus in turn curbs the food cravings for a longer time.

Green Fun

- 1 cup of spinach
- 1 avocado, pitted and peeled
- 1 kiwi fruit
- A dash of honey
- 1 teaspoon of lime juice
- 1 cup of coconut water

1. Blend the spinach with coconut water first.
2. Once smooth, add the kiwi fruit, avocado, lime juice and honey.
3. Blend. Serve chilled in glasses to enjoy.

Honey and kiwi fruit added to this smoothie completely take away the bitter taste of the spinach. This is a wonderfully nutritious smoothie, rich in both fibers, minerals, vitamins and antioxidants.

It's also tremendously low in calories and is therefore ideal for even frequent consumption. It promotes weight loss without stripping the body off the essential minerals, vitamins and fats.

Creamy Ginger

- 1 whole apple, peeled
- 1 whole banana, peeled
- ½ inch ginger, peeled and crushed
- 1 peach
- 1 cup of coconut milk

1. Blend the apple and banana slices with coconut milk.
2. Add the peach and crushed ginger.
3. Drop in a few ice cubes and enjoy.

Weight loss isn't about just consuming less calories and indulging in performing cardio workouts. Weight loss is much more than that and involves boosting the body's nutrient absorption capability as well. Ginger provides an all round support for weight loss. Not only does it helps to curb the hunger pangs, keeping the digestive system healthy and active but enhances the nutrient absorption capability of the body. Proper absorption of nutrients helps to keep the system feeling full for longer, thus keeping unnecessary hunger at bay. Moreover, ginger also helps relieve muscle stress and tiredness which happens as a result of working out, thus ensuring that the weight loss plan is maintained.

Spiced Veggies

- 1 whole head of broccoli
- ½ cup of kale
- 1 whole carrot, peeled and halved
- 1 turnip
- 1 inch cinnamon, crushed
- 1 teaspoon of honey
- 1 cup of coconut water

1. First blend the spinach with coconut water.
2. Add the carrot, turnip, crushed cinnamon and broccoli. Blend again until smooth.
3. Finish off by mixing honey and tossing in some ice cubes.

Veggies are perfect and also essential for weight loss. Consuming green smoothies is a must. You will never feel even a hunch with this one. Cinnamon and honey present in this smoothie give it an excellent and unique taste and also take away the commonly occurring bitterness of smoothies. On the contrary, everything that had been included in this smoothie, ranging from honey to the vegetables, helps to keep the body fit and active.

Peachy Popsicle

- 1 whole banana
- 1 teaspoon of fresh lemon juice
- 1 whole peach
- 4 maraschino cherries
- 1 cup of cantaloupe, cubed
- 1 cup of coconut milk

1. Blend all the fruits with coconut milk.
2. Stir in lemon juice and serve chilled.

Creamy and enriching, Peachy Popsicle is one of those smoothies which will make you completely forget that you are on weight loss program. Lemon juice present in this smoothie helps promote weight loss by normalizing the digestive system and boosting excretion of excess fat from the body. On the contrary, peaches being low in sodium content help reduce water retention and bloating.

Plum-ed Up

- 3 whole plums, seeded
- 4 cherries, fresh
- 1 cup of coconut water
- 4 strawberries
- 1 egg
- 1 whole green cardamom, peeled and crushed

1. Blend the strawberries, plums and cherries with the coconut water.
2. Blend the crushed cardamom and egg with the rest of the things.
3. So serve chilled, add a few ice cubes.

Egg enriched smoothies are one of my favorites. As against the common saying goes that eggs add on to weight gain, fat and cholesterol present in eggs help fight the bad cholesterol instead of adding on to weight. Other than eggs, the plums also help to promote weight loss. Plums are rich in vitamin C or citric acid, which can relieve muscle sprain and tiredness thereby enabling the person to get involved in heavy workouts on a regular basis and lose weight effectively and naturally.

Cantaloupe County

- 1 whole cantaloupe, cubed
- 1 banana
- 1 egg
- 2 cups of coconut milk
- 1 peach

1. Blend the fruits with coconut milk.
2. Blend the egg.
3. Serve chilled.

Cantaloupes may not be that popular as apples and oranges, it is surprisingly a super food for weight loss. One large cantaloupe is known to provide about 265 calories, which can easily substitute for other filling calorie laden foods. Other than that, it also provides the body with a variety of vitamins like vitamin C, minerals and the most shocking thing is omega 3 fatty acids!

Cantaloupe is also one of those fruits which get digested very fast, thus keeping digestion problems at bay. This smoothie is ideal for post workout duration and you will simply never get bored with this smoothie.

Beach Breeze

- 1 cup of coconut water
- 1 banana
- 1 cup of pineapple chunks
- 1 whole mango
- 7-8 lychees, seeded
- 1 nectarine
- 1 cup of watermelon

1. Seed the mango, watermelon and lychees.
2. Blend all the fruits with coconut water.
3. Serve with ice cubes.

A perfectly beach based concoction of tropical fruits, this smoothie will make you feel like you are in heaven. It is unbelievably low in calories, yet filling and provides the body with fibers, vitamins and minerals which are crucial for proper and faster weight loss.

Bunch of Roses

- 7-8 strawberries
- 7-8 cherries
- 1/2 cup of watermelon, cubed
- 2 figs
- 1 cup of coconut water

1. Blend the fruits with coconut water until smooth.
2. Serve chilled.

Red is my favorite color, but that is not the only reason for me to be in love with this smoothie. Its clear like a juice and doesn't makes me feel heavy at any point. However; the high water content and fiber level of these fruits keep me full for an unbelievably long duration. Just blend it all together and you will be satiated within seconds.

Pretty Peach

- 1 peach
- 1 mango
- 4 strawberries
- 1 banana
- 1 cup of coconut milk
- 1 nectarine

1. Blend the peeled banana, mango, peach, nectarine and strawberries with the coconut milk.
2. Blend until smooth.
3. Serve immediately or refrigerate.

Peach, mango, strawberries, nectarine and banana; oh, I love fruits and especially the ones that are juicy and filling. Banana and peaches provide me the essential fibers to keep my body healthy, active and going and the strawberries keep me full due to their high water content. I simply love imagining treating myself to this smoothie.

Wonder Veggies

- 1 cup of spinach
- 1 turnip
- 1 radish
- 1 red bell pepper, seeded and chopped
- 1 inch ginger
- 1 glass of water

1. First blend the spinach and ginger with water.
2. Then blend in the red bell pepper, turnip and radish.
3. Once ready, enjoy the spicy veggie smoothie.

This smoothie is a complete detox but all you have to do get it is to blend this easily available, inexpensive veggies together and drink the smoothie. Although you may not be loving it at the first sip, you will soon feel blessed and will be blessing this smoothie as well.

Amazing Avocado

- 1 banana
- 1 avocado, peeled and pitted
- 1 teaspoon of lemon juice
- 1 glass of coconut milk

1. Blend the fruits with the coconut milk.
2. Blend in lemon juice.
3. Serve with ice cubes and enjoy.

Did you know that avocado and banana are two fruits that are included in the list of foods which get digested fastest?

Nutty Toast

- 5-6 cashew nuts
- 1 mango
- 5-6 walnuts
- 1 carrot
- 1 cup of coconut water

1. Blend the carrot and nuts with coconut water.
2. Blend the mango.
3. Serve to enjoy.

Mango and cashew nuts both are considered bad for weight loss. However; the fact is that both these things are far better than calorie laden foods and satisfy hunger without even adding on to the fat and cholesterol levels considerably. Hence; you should not hesitate having this smoothie.

Daring Desire

- 1 cup of blueberries
- ½ cup of blackberries
- 5 black currants
- 1 teaspoon of honey
- 1 cup of coconut milk

1. Drop all the fruits in the blender.
2. Add coconut milk. Blend to mix.
3. Serve and enjoy.

This smoothie sure stands up to its name. Black currants are a great addition not only because they improve the taste of the smoothie but also because these make it just perfect for weight loss. So, enjoy.

Pleasant Pear

- 1 pear
- 1 banana
- 1 apple
- 1 glass of coconut water
- 2 dates, pitted

1. Pour coconut water into blender.
2. Add the fruits and dates.
3. Blend, serve and enjoy the smoothie chilled.

Pear is yet another favorite fruits of mine. Its teasing taste is heavenly for my taste buds and also helps me lose weight while eating deliciously. Pear is also rich in fibers and vitamins, which makes weight loss process a better experience.

Chapter 4 Paleo Diet During Your Weight-Loss Program – How to Stay Motivated and Get Lean with Smoothies

Motivation is something that is necessary to have in order to begin a process of change. It is also a necessary component of maintaining those changes. As you see the weight disappearing, the smaller clothes fitting and experience surges in energy levels and overall health, you will be motivated to keep up this lifestyle. Why? You will see and feel it working. There is nothing more motivating than success!

The addition of smoothies in your paleo diet will help you to remain motivated for the long term because you will not be beating yourself up for falling off of the Paleolithic wagon. They empower you to be able to crush cravings for foods that will ruin your progress. The more you empower yourself, the more motivation you will have to successfully continue living paleo.

As you venture further and further along the paleo-path, you may want to diversify your smoothies. This can be done several ways, and as long as you stick to the foods you are supposed to be eating.

1. Mix and match ingredients. Try to stick with one fruit, and the rest veggies. Mix and match what sounds good to you. Add herbs, splashes of flavor, and fats. Experimentation can be fun and interesting.

2. Put your smoothie in the freezer and allow it to firm up. Eat it with a spoon. It will trick you into feeling more like you are eating a desert and makes a great substitute for ice cream!

3. Use fancy glassware. Buy pretty ice-tea, sundae, and other glasses to drink your smoothies from. It will be visually appealing! Store your glasses in the freezer.

4. Add sprigs of herbs or slices of fruit to add even more visual appeal. It makes the smoothie a real special treat when you take the time to make it pretty!

Smoothies make a great meal replacement if you add enough vegetables. If you consider the fact that a salad can be a meal, so can a smoothie. It will allow you to pack in a ton of vitamins and nutrients without a ton of calories. This is especially helpful when you're on the go. You can get things done while drinking your breakfast, lunch or dinner.

As long as you keep paleo interesting, it is easy to stick with. You will be seeing and feeling the fruits of your labor on a regular basis. There is nothing more motivating than results and success. By incorporating smoothies into your paleo lifestyle, you will help to ensure that you have an endless amount of motivation!

Conclusion

Thank you again for downloading this book!

I hope this book was able to get you excited about starting your weight loss venture by adhering to a Paleo-lifestyle using delicious smoothies to keep you on track!

I want to congratulate you for making the right decision to lose weight and keep it off. Paleolithic living will allow you to achieve both while helping your body to function at its finest. The journey that you are about to embark on is exciting, fulfilling and will bring you health and happiness.

Now that you are equipped with the ins and outs of the Paleo diet, including food lists and smoothie recipes, you are well prepared to successfully achieve all of your weight loss goals. Do not waste another second. Clean out your kitchen and rid your life of all the foods that are making you fat and unhealthy. Run to the store and get all the fresh organic produce and meats that you can stuff in your cart!

A major part of staying on track with the Paleo method is the ability to say no to cravings. The smoothie recipes will help you to do just that. You will be able to crush your cravings while powering down delicious, healthy, hydrating smoothies.

Grab your blender and ingredients and get started. You will satiate your palate, impress friends and family, all while improving your health and losing weight. Maximizing your produce intake with the use of smoothies is the greatest idea since sliced bread (a paleo-no-no)!

I hope that the information in this book proves to be as useful for you as it was for me in losing weight the paleo-way. You have all the tools needed to be successful. Get started today. Achieve weight loss and keep it off. You can do it!

Finally, if you enjoyed this book, please take the few minutes to share your thoughts and post a review on Amazon. It would be greatly appreciated!

Thank you and GOOD LUCK!

Recommended Reading For You

You may also want to check my other books:

-> Gluten-Free Vegan Cookbook: 90+ Healthy, Easy and Delicious Recipes for Vegan Breakfasts, Salads, Soups, Lunches, Dinners and Desserts – Annette Goodman

90+ Healthy, Easy and Delicious Recipes for Vegan Breakfasts, Salads, Soups, Lunches, Dinners and Desserts for Your Well-Being + Shopping List To Save Your Precious Time

Gluten-Free Vegan diet doesn't have to be bland and boring at all! These recipes are original, easy to make and just delightfully appetizing. They will enrich your culinary experience and let you enjoy your breakfasts, lunches, dinners and desserts with your friends and family.

In this book you will find:

-23 Scrumptious and Easy Breakfasts
-27 Delicious and Savory Lunches and Dinners
-22 Aromatic And Nutritious Soups
-21 Enticing And Rich Desserts
-Extra Shopping List to Save Your Precious Time
= 93 Fantastic Gluten-Free Healthy Vegan Recipes!
The Gluten-Free diet will help you detoxify, improve your immune system and make you feel younger - both mentally and physically! The Change is just in front of you!

Direct Buy Link: http://www.amazon.com/dp/B00LU915YA/

-> Fast Freezer Meals: Delicious and Quick Gluten-Free Slow Cooker Recipes for Make-Ahead Meals That Will Save Your Time and Improve Your Health

Discover Delicious and Quick Gluten-Free Slow Cooker Recipes for Make-Ahead Meals That Will Save Your Time and Improve Your Health!

As a person diagnosed with coeliac disease I had to soon come up with an efficient strategy that would enable me to maintain my gluten-free diet while handling work, kids, house, sport and all the other areas of my life at the same time. That wasn't easy, and that's why I'm here to give you a helpful hand. Even if you're not diagnosed or gluten intolerant, these recipes will just make you healthier and more energetic.

Most of these recipes can be prepared in no more than 30 minutes and then just effortlessly cooked in your crockpot when you're at work or doing your business!

Direct Buy Link: http://www.amazon.com/dp/B00M783PS2/

-> Gluten Free Crock Pot Recipes: Healthy, Easy and Delicious Slow Cooker Paleo Recipes for Breakfast, Lunch and Dinner
Discover Healthy, Easy and Delicious Slow Cooker Paleo Recipes for Breakfast, Lunch and Dinner for You and Your Family!

Save your time and start healthy living with these delectable slow cooker gluten free recipes tailor-made for busy people!

I've been on the Gluten Free diet for more than ten years now!
Although the main reason for my radical diet change was my diagnosis (Coeliac disease), I would never-ever (even if given a magical chance) take the lane of eating gluten again!

Direct Buy Link: http://www.amazon.com/dp/B00K5UVYUA/

-> Anti Inflammatory Diet: Beginner's Guide: What You Need To Know To Heal Yourself with Food + Recipes + One Week Diet Plan

"He who takes medicine and neglects to diet wastes the skill of his doctors." - *Chinese Proverb*

Are you suffering from the severe symptoms that you've been trying to overcome for a long time now using your prescribed pills, but just stuck somewhere in the middle?

Unrestrained inflammation lead to asthma, allergies, tissue and cell degeneration, heart diseases, cancer and various other maladies, which are difficult to deal with.
I myself suffered from long and gruesome periods of acute inflammation. I had the IBS symptoms and very bad, extremely painful sinusitis. It started to affect my day to day ability to work and my potential and productivity suffered a steep decline. Medication helped but the effect was only temporary. I would be confined to my house for days without any solution to my problem. Every doctor I visited could pinpoint the superficial problem and treat it but none could tell me what was causing this problem, time after time.
And the problem was my diet!

Vast majority of the recipes I included in this book can be prepared really fast and easily! I also included absolutely delicious One Week Diet Plan for you!

->Direct Buy Link: http://www.amazon.com/dp/B00MQ9HI58/

***

You may also want to download my friend's books.

Help your mind today with these:

- NLP: Improve Your Relationship Fast:
http://www.amazon.com/dp/B00J70HWYG/
- NLP: Gain Self-Confidence Fast:

http://www.amazon.com/dp/B00IEJSJ0C/

- NLP: Stress Management:

http://www.amazon.com/dp/B00JGVZ8L0/

- Buddhism: Beginner's Guide – #1 Amazon Bestseller in 3 categories:

http://www.amazon.com/dp/B00MHSR5YM/

- Meditation: Beginner's Guide:

http://www.amazon.com/ dp/B00KQRU9BC/

<u>My Mailing list</u>: If you would like to receive **new Kindle reads** on **wellness, gluten free diet, social dynamics, psychology, career, NLP, success and healthy living** for **FREE** (or deeply **discounted – as low as $0,99**) <u>I invite you to my Mailing List.</u> Whenever my new book is out, I set the promotional price/free period for two days. You will get an e-mail notification and will **be the first to get the book for $0,99 (or free)** during its limited promotion.

Why would I do this when it took me countless hours to write these e-books?

First of all, that's my way of saying **"thank you"** to my new readers. Second of all – **I want to spread the word about my new books and ideas.** Mind you that **I hate spam and e-mails that come too frequently** - no worries about that.

If you think that's a good idea and are in, just follow this link:

http://eepurl.com/R_UhP

You may also like us on Facebook:

www.facebook.com/HolisticWellnessBooks

We have created this page with a few fellow authors of mine. We hope you find it inspiring and helpful.

Thank You for your time and interest in our work!

Annette Goodman & Holistic Wellness eBooks

About The Author

Hello! My name is Annette Goodman. I'm glad we met. Who am I? A homegrown cook, gluten-free diet follower, successful wellness aficionado and a writer. I live in Portland, Oregon with my husband, son and our dear golden retriever, Fluffy. I work as a retail manager in of the European companies. My entire childhood I suffered from obesity, hypertension and complexion problems. During my college years I decided to turn my life around and started my weight-loss and wellness pursue. After more than a decade I can say that I definitely succeeded and now I'd like to give you a hand. I love cooking, creating new healthy recipes and writing books about healthy lifestyle for you to enjoy and profit from. I hope we'll meet again!

Printed in Great Britain
by Amazon